I Can Help

Written by Anthony Robinson
Illustrated by Kate Leake

Collins

Helping my family is fun.

2

3

I can help in the kitchen.

I can help in the garden.

I can help to wash the car.

I can help at bath time ...

11

Helping makes me sleepy!

13

Helping

Ideas for reading

Written by Clare Dowdall, PhD
Lecturer and Primary Literacy Consultant

Reading objectives:
- use phonic knowledge to decode regular words and read them aloud accurately
- use phonic knowledge to decode regular words and read them aloud accurately
- demonstrate understanding when talking with others about what they have read

Communication and language objectives:
- answer "how" and "why" questions about their experiences and in response to stories or events
- express themselves effectively, showing awareness of listeners' needs

- listen to stories, accurately anticipating key events and respond to what they hear with relevant comments, questions or actions

Curriculum links: Personal, Social and Emotional Development

High frequency words: I, can, in, is, the, to, at, me

Interest words: helping, family, kitchen, garden, wash, car, bath time, sleepy

Word count: 34

Build a context for reading

- Invite children to give examples of how they help at home, and why it is good to help others.

- Look at the front and back covers together. Ask the children in pairs to read the title and the blurb, and to describe what is happening in the pictures.

- Ask children to share their ideas and to predict how the child is going to help in the story.

Understand and apply reading strategies

- Read pp2–3 together. Look at the word *helping*. Show children how to sound it out, e.g. *h-e-l-p-i-ng*.

- Ask children to tell a partner about how the boy is helping his family in the pictures on pp2–3.

- Ask children to read the story independently and aloud to the end, looking for how the boy is helping each time.

- Support children as they read, moving around the group and intervening where necessary to praise, encourage and help.